The World
Has Need
of You

The World Has Need of You

Poems for Connection

INTRODUCTION BY ALBERTO RÍOS

COPPER CANYON PRESS

PORT TOWNSEND, WASHINGTON

Cover design by Phil Kovacevich

Copper Canyon Press is in residence at Fort Worden State Park in Port Townsend, Washington, under the auspices of Centrum. Centrum is a gathering place for artists and creative thinkers from around the world, students of all ages and backgrounds, and audiences seeking extraordinary cultural enrichment.

LIBRARY OF CONGRESS CONTROL NUMBER: 2023932395
ISBN 978-1-55659-623-0

COPPER CANYON PRESS
Post Office Box 271
Port Townsend, Washington 98368
www.coppercanyonpress.org

Contents

Preface

> The stars don't know which constellation they're in.
>
> JAMES RICHARDSON

Shortly after the COVID-19 pandemic struck, and throughout months of protest and calls for racial justice, the staff and board of directors at Copper Canyon Press gathered to determine how we might proceed—how, amid so much uncertainty, we might maintain our connection to one another, to our poets, and to our readers. Our home state of Washington was the first hotspot in the United States, and we experienced a fear and uncertainty that has become all too familiar around the globe. Unable to meet in person, we gathered via video conference to read poems together. Simple as that. Each of us, sitting in the fortunate comfort of our own homes, took turns and engaged what the poet Hayden Carruth called "the voice that is great within us." Poetry is famously different from news reporting or what is found in board and meeting rooms. And yet, just like data mining or legal contracts, newsfeeds or therapeutic counseling, poetry offers us a necessary way to approach, enter, and face the uncertainty of the moment.

Our nonprofit mission affirms that poetry "is vital to living and learning," and that affirmation found a real-life application from the first moment we gathered, each in our isolation, each moving toward greater connection through an engagement with poetry. The poems we shared proved useful and helpful, we listened to one another and paid attention in new and surprising ways. One of us read Ellen Bass's "The World Has Need of You" and tears rose. Clearly we needed these poems, and so over the course of the next few weeks we gathered many poems and began posting them on our website.

While the experience of a poem is individual, a book of poems, particularly an anthology of poems, is a gathering of voices into a constellation's larger story. As an organization, we came to recognize how the poets and poems we've published over nearly fifty years were once again speaking to us, sustaining us, and urging us onward. Like stars, poems do not know what sort of organization they might be drawn into, or what sort of constellation might offer them a larger narrative, yet through poems we at Copper Canyon Press have come to see a connection between poems, between readers, between you and me, between individual imaginations.

This slender anthology represents a coming together of imaginations and aspirations; it's a belief in the lived experience of individuals who have tried to make sense of uncertainty even while embracing the uncertainty at the core of living.

My thanks to editors Elaina Ellis and John Pierce for assembling the final selection of poems, and to Emily Grise, our digital content manager, for managing the online version on our website.

Thank you for being a part of Copper Canyon Press—thank you for reading, for being safe, for being kind. We hope you find even more in the stars than we might have previously imagined.

Michael Wiegers
Executive Editor
Copper Canyon Press

Introduction

ALBERTO RÍOS

Wild days. I know. We all know.

Black Lives Matter. COVID-19, the pandemic, social distancing. The economy. The border, in all things. The lifespan of Supreme Court justices. Aches and pains. Loneliness. Mosquito bites. Horror and bad dreams and imagination. Boredom. Rain. The list starts big but immediately leads to things no less real or important in the actual experience of our daily lives— what makes up the live-a-day mundane. All this and some happiness, too.

At this pivotal moment in history, with so many issues vying mightily for our attention, we are suffering from a matrix of emotions tethered to an array of options—which sounds good but is not always a healthy combination. Complexity is our human condition, and it is always the first part of the mix. The world is simply strange, and we must work very hard to understand that strangeness or else be overwhelmed by it. In that strangeness, though, I still think there's a little bit of magic. It's shy, and you have to look for it. And with so much that is loud in the world, there sometimes seems to be no room for it.

What is it that we want? A perfect world, of course. More pragmatically, a perfect union. We have thought that union to be geographic, but it turns out to be psychological and sociological as well—we are individual human beings, finally, living together. We often think that a perfect world is one in which everyone understands and reacts to the world as we do. It seems so self-evident. That said, difference is a curious animal, and poets are the ones who can carefully and painstakingly lead us to other places, helping us all as readers to see, to feel, to experience the senses in alternative contexts. We come through it all even more alive for how our imaginations are fed by possibility and nuance.

Poets feed us. They look where there seems to be nothing to see, and they see. They see and they report, sometimes rashly, sometimes elegantly, sometimes in ways that have no name. Underscoring what poetry does is a sense of *somethingness:* of power, of undertow, of quietude, of importance. Even though we did not see these forces before, we see them after a poem, or a story, or an essay, or a song. We are gifted by them with something more in our lives.

I often ask my young audiences who the most powerful wizard in the Harry Potter series is. We might be tempted to say Dumbledore or Lord Voldemort or Harry himself. But the answer turns out to be simple and unequivocal. The most powerful wizard in the Harry Potter universe—in any writing—is the author. The author turns out to be everything. Dracula is not powerful, ultimately; Bram Stoker is. Mr. Hyde is made powerful by Robert Louis Stevenson.

Although Harry and the other wizards cast spells with their magic wands, the real magic wand is the pencil that belongs to the author. Indeed, a *spell* and *spelling* come from related etymologies. To spell a word correctly is to ask it to come forward out of a million other words and do your bidding. This is a powerful moment, even if we don't recognize the value of good spelling in a grocery list. In visiting schools and giving talks through the years, I have always said, "Every pencil is filled with a book." And as things turn out, a regular no. 2 pencil has enough lead to write about 45,000 words—a small novel.

Whatever writing implement authors choose, their pencil is, at its heart, a magic wand, and writers are promoted to wizards in its debt. Understanding that what poets imagine is passed from them through the pencil to the page makes the magic in all books far more reachable, more touchable, more palpable, and more possible than we suppose. Writers think a world into being.

There are 1,084,170 words in the Harry Potter series—that constitutes a little more than the use of twenty-four pencils. This math is fanciful, perhaps, and authors are more likely use a computer, but the underlying fact of this metaphor remains clear. Twenty-four pencils. Writers are the makers of the magic, and now more than ever need to be. They are the speakers of our time. Poets in particular: they are the wrestlers of dream.

Wild days indeed. Sadness, happiness, and all the heroic gray in between. These are our lives. We are here and the moment is ours to meet. Our actions, in a very real way, are the pathway to whatever future awaits us. The world simply will not be the same as it was, and what will be changed is up to us.

Go on, go out onto the wild, wild page. Find your words—writing, reading, singing. Find your words.

The World
Has Need
of You

CHASE TWICHELL

You, Reader, as I Imagine You

Why is it awkward to acknowledge
each other's presence here?

Who says we can't meet in public,
can't stop and sit together on a bench
and watch the dogs go by?

As a child, I looked for you
in books and sometimes sensed
you (reading what I was reading).

Even as a child I knew you would
someday come to this place to meet me.

MARIANNE BORUCH

All of Us All of Us

Anyone could stand in a kitchen, tiny
barbs of arrow sinking
in again. Whoever shot it good
missed the heart.

That's the problem, isn't it? The only partly.
Brave and pathetic the way we
walk away okay enough, and think things.

Something fated to be given, but not gotten.
Something dreamt never coming with, on waking.
No longer no longer no longer something.

It's the repeat—how a car
can drive the same road home, years
the ruts, the standing water every spring.
It can make you sick because
you wanted to love it.

To keep the already said going,
to sit then rise again. And to
leave in the sink: the cup with a little coffee,
lettuce on a plate from lunch.
All of us, all of us.
Even anguish in such small things is

everyone singing.

Rain Light

All day the stars watch from long ago
my mother said I am going now
when you are alone you will be all right
whether or not you know you will know
look at the old house in the dawn rain
all the flowers are forms of water
the sun reminds them through a white cloud
touches the patchwork spread on the hill
the washed colors of the afterlife
that lived there long before you were born
see how they wake without a question
even though the whole world is burning

CAMILLE RANKINE

The Current Isolationism

In the half-light, I am most
at home, my shadow
as company.

When I feel hot, I push a button
to make it stop. I mean this stain on my mind
I can't get out. How human

I seem. Like modern man,
I traffic in extinction. I have a gift.
Like an animal, I sustain.

A flock of birds
when touched, I scatter. I won't approach
until the back is turned.

My heart betrays. I confess: I am afraid.
How selfish of me.
When there's no one here, I halve

the distance between
our bodies infinitesimally.
In this long passageway, I pose

against the wallpaper, dig
my heels in, catch the light.
In my vision, the back door opens

on a garden that is always
in bloom. The dogs
are chained so they can't attack like I know

they want to. In the next yard
over, honeybees swarm
and their sound is huge.

OLAV HAUGE

Anxiety

There's nervous energy in everything now: anxiety in the sunlight,
anxiety in the stars, anxiety in the earth, anxiety
in the grass, the hornets' nest, tension
in both men and women, friction
in cars, planes, and wires,
a charge in the stove,
the coffeepot,
the cat—
jolt, jolt, jolt,
there's current
in everything one touches,
Olai claims.
That's why he stands in rubber boots,
digging himself down
to the blue clay, the cold water.

SARAH RUHL

Prayer

Let the day open slow around you.
Let the night open slow around you.

Let the spring open slow
the fall open slow
the waking animals open their eyes slow
around you.

Let the night close slow around you.
Let the day close slow around you.

The winter close slow
the summer close slow
the sleeping animals close their eyes slow
around you.

ARTHUR SZE

Unpacking a Globe

I gaze at the Pacific and don't expect
to ever see the heads on Easter Island,

though I guess at sunlight rippling
the yellow grasses sloping to shore;

yesterday a doe ate grass in the orchard:
it lifted its ears and stopped eating

when it sensed us watching from
a glass hallway—in his sleep, a veteran

sweats, defusing a land mine.
On the globe, I mark the Battle of

the Coral Sea—no one frets at that now.
A poem can never be too dark,

I nod and, staring at the Kenai, hear
ice breaking up along an inlet;

yesterday a coyote trotted across
my headlights and turned his head

but didn't break stride; that's how
I want to live on this planet:

alive to a rabbit at a glass door—
and flower where there is no flower.

DAVID BUDBILL

What Issa Heard

Two hundred years ago Issa heard the morning birds
singing sutras to this suffering world.

I heard them too, this morning, which must mean,

since we will always have a suffering world,
we must also always have a song.

LUCILLE CLIFTON

won't you celebrate with me

won't you celebrate with me
what i have shaped into
a kind of life? i had no model.
born in babylon
both nonwhite and woman
what did i see to be except myself?
i made it up
here on this bridge between
starshine and clay,
my one hand holding tight
my other hand; come celebrate
with me that everyday
something has tried to kill me
and has failed.

RACHEL MCKIBBENS

letter from my heart to my brain

It's okay to hang upside down
like a bat, to swim
into the deep end of silence,
to swallow every key
so you can't get out.

It's okay to hear the ocean
calling your fevered name,
to say your sorrow is an opera
of snakes, to flirt with sharp
& heartless things.

It's okay to write,
I deserve everything!
To bow down
to this rotten thing
that understands you,
to adore the red
& ugly queen of it, admire
her calm & steady rowing.

It's okay to lock yourself
in the medicine cabinet,
to drink all the wine,
to do what it takes
to stay without staying.

It's okay to hate
God today, to change
his name to yours,
to want to ruin all
that ruined you.

It's okay to feel
like only a photograph
of yourself, to need
a stranger to pull
your hair & pin you down,

it's okay to want
your mother
as you lie alone
in bed.

It's okay to brick
to fuck to flame
to church to crush
to knife to rock
& rock & rock
& rock
& rock & rock
& rock.

It's okay to wave
goodbye to yourself
in the mirror.

To write, *I don't want anything.*
It's okay to despise
what you have inherited,
to feel dead
in a city of pulses.

It's okay to be the whale
that never comes up
for air, to love best
the taste of your
own blood.

Who I Write For

I

Historians and newsmen and people who are just curious ask me,
Who am I writing for?

I'm not writing for the gentleman in the stuffy coat, or for his offend-
ed moustache, not even for the warning finger he raises in the sad
ripples of music.

Not for the lady hidden in her carriage (her lorgnette sending its cold
light through the windowpanes).

Perhaps I write for people who don't read my poems. That woman
who dashes down the street as if she had to open the doors for the
sunrise.

Or that old fellow nodding on a bench in the little park while the
setting sun takes him with love, wraps him up and dissolves him,
gently, in its light.

For everyone who doesn't read my writing, all the people who don't
care about me (though they care for me, without knowing).

The little girl who glances my way as she passes, my companion on
this adventure, living in the world.

And the old woman who sat in her doorway and watched life and
bore many lives and many weary hands.

I write for the man who's in love. For the man who walks by with
his pain in his eyes. The man who listened to him. The man who
looked away as he walked by. The man who finally collapsed when
he asked his question and no one listened.

I write for all of them. I write, mostly, for the people who don't
   read me. Each one and the whole crowd. For the breasts and the
   mouths and the ears, the ears that don't listen, but keep
my words alive.

II

But I also write for the murderer. For the man who shut his eyes and
   threw himself at somebody's heart and ate death instead of food
   and got up crazy.

For the man who puffed himself up into a tower of rage and then
   collapsed on the world.

For the dead woman and the dead children and dying men.

For the person who quietly turned on the gas and destroyed the
   whole city and the sun rose on a pile of bodies.

For the innocent girl with her smile, her heart, her sweet medallion
   (and a plundering army went through there).

And for the plundering army that charged into the sea and sank.

And for the waters, for the infinite sea.

No, not infinite. For the finite sea that has boundaries almost like our
   own, like a breathing lung.

(At this point a little boy comes in, jumps in the water, and the sea,
   the heart of the sea, is in his pulse!)

And for the last look, the hopelessly limited Last Look, in whose
   arms someone falls asleep.

Everyone's asleep. The murderer and the innocent victim, the boss
    and the baby, the damp and the dead, the dried-up old fig and the
    wild, bristling hair.

For the bully and the bullied, the good and the sad,
the voice with no substance
and all the substance of the world.

For you, the man with nothing that will turn into a god, who reads
    these words without desire.

For you and everything alive inside of you,
I write, and write.

Translated by Lewis Hyde

from 13th Balloon

What was that trick
How did you do it

It was as if you'd unfolded a map
you'd secretly been drawing
for us all along   a map
of a new and radiant country
across which together we would
carry you as you died

///

In truth I don't have that many
                    memories of you left
                    maybe enough
                    that were they spliced together
the result would be the length of a movie trailer
or if weighed
would weigh as much as an eggshell

I can remember some things you said
if not verbatim   the tone   the inflection
and whether they arrived through a phone line
or through the air
or whether you thought something
you were saying was funny
like the time near the end
when you told your favorite nurse
who was trying a new diet
that if she really wanted to lose
weight she should have sex with you
            C'mere lemme stick it in you
            you'll lose thirty pounds real quick

We lived on a planet of disaster
We lived in a country of misery
We lived in a state of horror
We lived in a city of scandal
We lived in a house of daily dying
from which to distract ourselves
we sometimes embroidered
the filthiest jokes we could think up
on every available towel   pillowcase   sheet
I shouldn't say it saved us
but in many ways it did

ANNA SWIR

There Is a Light in Me

Whether in daytime or in nighttime
I always carry inside
a light.
In the middle of noise and turmoil
I carry silence.
Always
I carry light and silence.

Duplex

I begin with love, hoping to end there.
I don't want to leave a messy corpse.

    I don't want to leave a messy corpse
    Full of medicines that turn in the sun.

Some of my medicines turn in the sun.
Some of us don't need hell to be good.

    Those who need most, need hell to be good.
    What are the symptoms of *your* sickness?

Here is one symptom of my sickness:
Men who love me are men who miss me.

    Men who leave me are men who miss me
    In the dream where I am an island.

In the dream where I am an island,
I grow green with hope. I'd like to end there.

LAO-TZU

Taoteching

8

The best are like water
bringing help to all
without competing
choosing what others avoid
they thus approach the Tao
dwelling with earth
thinking with depth
helping with kindness
speaking with honesty
governing with peace
working with skill
and moving with time
and because they don't compete
they aren't maligned

Translated by Red Pine

GHASSAN ZAQTAN

Fingers

What's that ringing in the brevity of silence,
delicate between destruction's instant
and fire's eruption?
Unrelenting and wise
fingers disassemble the horizon
into houses and send it back
to the beauty of dirt, iron, and people

Fingers that make the bed,
fold clothes, and organize photos
one garden at a time
so that peace may enter stone

Translated by Fady Joudah

DANA LEVIN

Urgent Care

Having to make eye contact
    with the economy—

A ball cap that says
    In Dog Years I'm Dead—"The moon

will turn *blood* red and then
    disappear for a while," the TV enthused. Hunched

over an anatomy textbook, a student
    traces a heart

    over another heart—lunar eclipse.

In the bathroom, crayoned
    graffiti:
        fuck the ♥

        —

He collected CAPTCHA, one seat over,
    Mr. feverish *Mange Denied:*

like *puzzling sabbath* or
    street pupas; we shared

some recent typos: *I'm*
    mediated (his), my *tiny bots*

of stimulation, he
    loved the smudged

and swoony words that proved him
    human—

not a machine trying to infiltrate
    the servers

of the *New York Times,* from which he launched
    (*gad shakes* or *hefty lama*)

obits and exposés, some recipes, a digital pic of someone else's
    black disaster, he

lobbed links at both of his fathers (step and bio),
    a few former lovers, a high school coach, a college chum, some people

"from where I used to work," so much info
    (we both agreed), "The umbra,"

the TV explained, shadow
    that Earth was about to make—

      —

    …and if during the parenthesis they felt a strange uneasiness…

    …firing rifles and clanging copper pots to rescue the threatened…

    …so benighted and hopelessly lost…

    …their eyes to the errors…

MOON LORE, *Farmers' Almanac.* Waiting room,
    hour two.

      —

Urgent Care. That was pretty
    multivalent. As in:

We really need you to take care of this.
We really need you

to care for this.
To care about this. We really need you

to peer through the clinic's
storefront window, on alert

for the ballyhooed moon—

And there it was. Reddening

in its black sock, deep
in the middle of the hour, of someone's

nutso-tinsel talk on splendor—

My fevered friend. Describing

the knocked-out flesh. Each of our heads
fitting like a flash drive

into the port of a healer's hands.

HAYDEN CARRUTH

Concerning Necessity

It's quite true we live
in a kind of rural twilight
most of the time giving
our love to the hard dirt
the water and the weeds
and the difficult woods

ho we say drive the wedge
heave the axe run the hand shovel
dig the potato patch
dig ashes dig gravel
tickle the dyspeptic chainsaw
make him snarl once more

while the henhouse needs cleaning
the fruitless corn to be cut
and the house is falling to pieces
the car coming apart
the boy sitting and complaining
about something everything anything

this was the world foreknown
though I had thought somehow
probably in the delusion
of that idiot Thoreau
that necessity could be saved
by the facts we actually have

like our extreme white birch
clasped in the hemlock's arms
or our baybreasted nuthatch
or our mountain and our stars
and really these things do serve
a little though not enough

what saves the undoubted collapse
of the driven day and the year
is my coming all at once
when she is done in or footsore
or down asleep in the field
or telling a song to a child

coming and seeing her move
in some particular way
that makes me to fall in love
all over with human beauty
the beauty I can't believe
right here where I live.

ALBERTO RÍOS

A Physics of Sudden Light

This is just about light, how suddenly
One comes upon it sometimes and is surprised.

In light, something is lifted.
That is the property of light,

And in it one weighs less.
A broad and wide leap of light

Encountered suddenly, for a moment—
You are not where you were

But you have not moved. It's the moment
That startles you up out of dream,

But the other way around: It's the moment, instead,
That startles you into dream, makes you

Close your eyes—that kind of light, the moment
For which, in our language, we have only

The word *surprise*, maybe a few others,
But not enough. The moment is regular

As with all the things regular
At the closing of the twentieth century:

A knowledge that electricity exists
Somewhere inside the walls;

That tonight the moon in some fashion will come out;
That cold water is good to drink.

The way taste slows a thing
On its way into the body.

Light, widened and slowed, so much of it: It
Cannot be swallowed into the mouth of the eye,

Into the throat of the pupil, there is
So much of it. But we let it in anyway,

Something in us knowing
The appropriate mechanism, the moment's lever.

Light, the slow moment of everything fast.
Like hills, those slowest waves, light,

That slowest fire, all
Confusion, confusion here

One more part of clarity: In this light
You are not where you were but you have not moved.

Obscurity and Lockdown

There was a spring at the top of the hill

water colder than it sounds once lying on his back

hands behind his head watching masses

of clouds push themselves around, once caught

a snake in the joe-pye weed about as big around

as an ankle monitor, once found a mess

of arrowheads above the calico bluffs; never minded

being by his own self, never minded his own

company; once he was a heller alright but he had

something, he had flow all by himself; once

he had a girl but this here wasn't enough not that

anyone ever asked not that anyone ever would, what

was it exactly he thought he was missing he would tell them

what: he missed kissing bigtime he missed kissing

Poema 18

Comes back from his blaze, the fireman,

from his star the astronomer,

from his disastrous passion the obsessive,

from one million whatever the ambitious,

from the naval night the sailor,

the poet returns from his slabber,

the soldier from fear,

the fisherman from his wet heart,

the mother from Juanito's fever,

the thief from his nighttime high,

the engineer from his frosted rose,

the native from his hunger,

the judge from fatigue and unsureness,

the jealous from his torment,

the dancer from her exhausted feet,

the architect from the three thousandth floor,

the pharaoh from his tenth life,

the hooker from her Lycra and falsies,

the hero comes back from oblivion,

the poor from another day gone,

the surgeon from staring down death,

the fighter from his pathetic contract,

someone returns from geometry,

stepping back from his infinity, the explorer,

the cook from her dirty dishes,

the novelist from a web of lies,

the hunter stamps out the fire and returns,

the adulterer from rapture and despair,

the professor from a glass of wine,

the schemer from his backstabbing,

the gardener has shuttered his rose,

the bartender stoppers his liquor,

the convict takes up his plea again,

the butcher washed his hands,

the nun quit her prayers,

the miner his slick tunnel,

and like the rest I take off my clothes,

inside the night of all men, I make

a smaller night for myself,

my woman joins me, silence bears down

and the dream spins the world again.

Translated by Forrest Gander

DEBORAH LANDAU

from Soft Targets

~

Don't blame the wisteria for setting off a feeling like freedom a feeling like joy.

We watched the people walking in the open square—

one of them was a specialist in killing, fear was the way of others.

I've seen the most extraordinary thing about people, their faces.

Remember the trees in springtime, we ate candy beneath them,

shouts from the playground, static of yellowjackets, your fresh new haircut.

Here's a tweeted canto, some words for the end of the world—

for when I am forever nothing, and you are

(and you and you).

What we were for such a brief.

(M with the laundry, the dog at his bowl, the boys going at it out back.)

O you who want to slaughter us, we'll be dead soon enough what's the rush

and this our only world.

Now bring me a souvenir from the desecrated city,

something tender, something that might bloom.

DAN GERBER

Often I Imagine the Earth

Often I imagine the earth
through the eyes of the atoms we're made of—
atoms, peculiar
atoms everywhere—
no me, no you, no opinions,
no beginning, no middle, no end,
soaring together like those
ancient Chinese birds
hatched miraculously with only one wing,
helping each other fly home.

Visitor

I am dreaming of a house just like this one

but larger and opener to the trees, nighter

than day and higher than noon, and you,

visiting, knocking to get in, hoping for icy

milk or hot tea or whatever it is you like.

For each night is a long drink in a short glass.

A drink of blacksound water, such a rush

and fall of lonesome no form can contain it.

And if it isn't night yet, though I seem to

recall that it is, then it is not for everyone.

Did you receive my invitation? It is not

for everyone. Please come to my house

lit by leaf light. It's like a book with bright

pages filled with flocks and glens and groves

and overlooked by Pan, that seductive satyr

in whom the fish is also cooked. A book that

took too long to read but minutes to unread—

that is—to forget. Strange are the pages

thus. Nothing but the hope of company.

I made too much pie in expectation. I was

hoping to sit with you in a treehouse in a

nightgown in a real way. Did you receive

my invitation? Written in haste, before

leaf blinked out, before the idea fully formed.

An idea like a stormcloud that does not spill

or arrive but moves silently in a direction.

Like a dark book in a long life with a vague

hope in a wood house with an open door.

Someday I'll Love Ocean Vuong

Ocean, don't be afraid.
The end of the road is so far ahead
it is already behind us.
Don't worry. Your father is only your father
until one of you forgets. Like how the spine
won't remember its wings
no matter how many times our knees
kiss the pavement. Ocean,
are you listening? The most beautiful part
of your body is wherever
your mother's shadow falls.
Here's the house with childhood
whittled down to a single red trip wire.
Don't worry. Just call it *horizon*
& you'll never reach it.
Here's today. Jump. I promise it's not
a lifeboat. Here's the man
whose arms are wide enough to gather
your leaving. & here the moment,
just after the lights go out, when you can still see
the faint torch between his legs.
How you use it again & again
to find your own hands.
You asked for a second chance
& are given a mouth to empty out of.
Don't be afraid, the gunfire
is only the sound of people
trying to live a little longer
& failing. Ocean. Ocean—
get up. The most beautiful part of your body
is where it's headed. & remember,
loneliness is still time spent
with the world. Here's

the room with everyone in it.
Your dead friends passing
through you like wind
through a wind chime. Here's a desk
with the gimp leg & a brick
to make it last. Yes, here's a room
so warm & blood-close,
I swear, you will wake—
& mistake these walls
for skin.

GREGORY ORR

"Not many of them, it's true"

Not many of them, it's true,
But certain poems
In an uncertain world—
The ones we cling to:

They bring us back
Always to the beloved
Whom we thought we'd lost.

As surely as if the words
Led her by the hand,
Brought him before us.

Certain poems
In an uncertain world.

ELLEN BASS

The World Has Need of You

everything here
seems to need us

RAINER MARIA RILKE

I can hardly imagine it
as I walk to the lighthouse, feeling the ancient
prayer of my arms swinging
in counterpoint to my feet.
Here I am, suspended
between the sidewalk and twilight,
the sky dimming so fast it seems alive.
What if you felt the invisible
tug between you and everything?
A boy on a bicycle rides by,
his white shirt open, flaring
behind him like wings.
It's a hard time to be human. We know too much
and too little. Does the breeze need us?
The cliffs? The gulls?
If you've managed to do one good thing,
the ocean doesn't care.
But when Newton's apple fell toward the earth,
the earth, ever so slightly, fell
toward the apple.

DEAN RADER

Meditation on Transmission

This poem appeared originally in the
San Francisco Chronicle on April 8, 2020.

The map on my
tv reddens the
way a wound
might spread
across skin,
here, the earth's
blue body brutally
infected, its slim
shape shrunken
somehow huddled,
like a child waiting
to be picked up,
held, carried to its
bed and sung to sleep,
in its dreams, death
comes dressed as a
doorknob, a handle
on a bus, a button,
a bowl of nuts,
the sun-stroked
sky, a whisper, a kiss,
and it says breath
of my breath, and it
says take me inside
you, and it says,
teach me to multiply,
and the earth
says, Look, I am
living, and the
earth says, holocene
and the earth

says, if something
isn't burning, it is
incubating, and
the waters do
not part, and
the sun does
not slide into
its black box,
and the stars
do not switch
off their light,
the rain does
not ask the
ocean for
water and yet
above a
chorus bristles
with birds about
their work
reminding
not everything
moving through
the air destroys.

JUNE JORDAN

Nobody Riding the Roads Today

Nobody riding the roads today
But I hear the living rush
far away from my heart

Nobody meeting on the streets
But I rage from the crowded
overtones of emptiness

Nobody sleeping in my bed
But I breathe like windows
broken by emergencies

Nobody laughing anymore
But I see the world split
and twisted up like open stone

Nobody riding the roads today
But I hear the living rush
far away from my heart

RUTH STONE

Goshen

For fifteen years I have lived in a house
without running water or furnace.
In and out the front door
with my buckets and armloads of wood.
This is the mountain.
This is the fortress of ice.
This is the stray cat skulking in the barn.
This is the barn with vacant windows
that lifts like a thin balsa kite
in the northeasters.
These are the winter birds
that wait in the bushes.
This is my measuring rod.
This is why I get up in the morning.
This is how I know where I am going.

LISA OLSTEIN

from A Poetics of Space

8. All These Constellations Are Yours

The ship dreams in terms of water.
Beautiful volume, the world stretches out.
Distant sails look like homing pigeons

whose wings once shone blue.
Little by little we take into our lungs
an echo. This is a way of saying

we do not see it start, yet it always starts
in the houses of the past, in the space of
elsewhere. We dream over a map,

desire describing a nation, a desert,
the plain or the plateau, the horizon
as much as the center. In the domain

under consideration, there are no young
forests. Honey in a hive is anything—
white nettle, blue sky. Space starts to dream

in the animal machine. Look in the eyes
of a trembling hare. The instant when
an animal that is all fear becomes lamb-like

calm is a proof: every atlas an absolute
elsewhere, the non-I woods,
the before-us forest.

Aphorisms and Ten-Second Essays

from Vectors 3.0:

If you can't take the first step, take the second.

from Vectors 4.2:

Faith is a kind of doubt ... of everything else. And doubt ... believes deeply it can do without believing.

More moving than someone weeping: someone trying not to.

Are these new storms, or has everything all together reached the age of falling down?

from Vectors 5.1:

I like having choices a lot better than using them.

HỒ XUÂN HƯƠNG

Country Scene

The waterfall plunges in mist.
Who can describe this desolate scene:

the long white river sliding through
the emerald shadows of the ancient canopy

… a shepherd's horn echoing in the valley,
fishnets stretched to dry on sandy flats.

A bell is tolling, fading, fading
just like love. Only poetry lasts.

                    Translated by John Balaban

JAMES ARTHUR

In Praise of Noise

The sound begins with a furnace
clicking awake in a two-room house, answered
by a few, then more, voices: gauges,

and old-fashioned watches ticking out of sync, in growing number,
so their *tip-tip-tip* fattens to a moan, joined

by a horn's upbeat honkity-honk, then ringtones and speakers
rehearsing drawn horsehair, air in a woodwind, or mimicking

a hand slapping a polyester drumhead, but unlike
these coarser frictions, playing the same, every time.
A car door bangs, a jackhammer hammers, and a bassline

purrs through a wall. The sound congeals,
sucking in more, a mechanical syrup in an IV drip, the automatic

ruckus of a robotic ocean, a symphony
no one wrote, confounding every pattern:

teach me the song that no one can sing, someday
to be the song of everything.

LAURA KASISCHKE

Masks

At the grocery store today—
these meteors and angels, wise men and all
the beautiful hallucinations of December, wearing
the masks of the Ordinary, the Annoyed, the Tired.
The Disturbed.
The Sane.

Only the recovering addict with his bucket and bell
has dared to come here without one.

He is Salvation.
His eyes have burned
holes in his radiance.
Instead of a mask, he has
unbuttoned his face.

JEAN VALENTINE

Even all night long

Even all night long while
the night train

pulls me on in my dream
like a needle

Even then, down in my bed
my hand across the sheet

anyone's hand
my face anyone's face

are held
and kissed

the water
the child

the friend
unlost.

ROGER REEVES

On Visiting the Site of a Slave Massacre in Opelousas

Grief, according to Dr. Johnson, *is a species of idleness.*
Then let me be idle—idle as one thousand orphaned oars,
vessel-less and beached in this cornfield, idle as a field
of black women underneath the hoof and boot of a swarm
of stallions robed in wedding gowns—not a bride among
them. I will mourn for what fails here—the deer, there,
dead in the ravine—the bees latching combs of honey
to its larynx, lungs, and breast. This is the idol of idle—
the bees harvesting honey in the good and rotting meat,
the drone's body, still in the last pitches of pleasure, taken
from the queen's chamber and cast from the hive by the workers—
the deer unaware of the work being done in its still body.
Sometimes, we entertain angels and violent strangers unawares.
You should know *nothing you love will be spared.* Mercy, yes mercy
is at the end of grief. It is somewhere between the deer's body
collapsing on the hive and one thousand bees galloping
against one another's needle-hung bodies in hopes of not being
the last to die. Isn't that what we pray for: misery, anywhere but here?

from I Am a Miner. The Light Burns Blue.

I am   thinking   about happiness again   how

you are in some   alternate orthography   perhaps you

are the   raised bumps in braille   perhaps your presence

allows   me to   examine the low   pressure area

the part that often   brings rain   without the clapping

and the   murmurs that are you   how would I see an

echo   as   anything   other than grieving light is here but

it is a   complement   what is the sun but   a source of

light and   what is   light   but a wavelength   detectable by

the eye   light is not   happiness   I seek the underside

of you   the mossy   dark follicle side   light includes

everything   it is perfectly   bound   and because perfect

darkness is   impossible   to create   I seek it as an eye

seeks the   black   cavity of   another eye

TED KOOSER

Right Hand

This old hand with which I am writing,
holding its pen and pecking its way
across the paper like a hen, has pulled me,
clucking with little discoveries,
across more than seventy years, a sometimes
muddy, sometimes frozen barnyard
where, looking back, it seems that every day
was rich with interest, both underfoot
and just an inch or two ahead of that.

AIMEE NEZHUKUMATATHIL

Love in the Time of Swine Flu

Because we think I might have it,
you take the couch. I can count on one hand
the times we have ever slept apart
under the same roof in our five years,

and those usually involved something
much worse than this sort of impenetrable
cough, the general misery involved
with dopey nausea, these vague chills.

But this time, we can't risk it—our small son
still breathes clear-light in the next room
and we can't afford to be *both* laid
up on our backs with a box of tissues

at our sides. Especially now that I carry
a small grapefruit, a second son, inside me.
In bed, I fever for your strong calves,
your nightsong breath on my neck

and—depending where we end up—wrist
or knee. I fever for the slip of straps down
my shoulder, I fever for the prickled pain
of lip-bite and bed burn. You get up and come

back to bed. We decide it is worth it. I wish
my name meant wing. The child still forming
inside me fevers for quiet, the silence of the after,
the silence of cell-bloom within our blood.

LUCIA PERILLO

For the First Crow with West Nile Virus
to Arrive in Our State

For a long time you lay tipped on your side like a bicycle
but now your pedaling has stopped. Already
the mosquitoes have chugged their blisterful of blood
and flown on. Time moves forward,
no cause to weep, I keep reminding myself of this:
the body will accrue its symptoms. And the handbooks,
which warn us not to use the absolutes, are wrong:
the body will *always* accrue its symptoms.

But shouldn't there also be some hatchlings within view:
sufficient birth to countervail the death?
At least a zero on the bottom line:
I'm not asking for black integers,
just for nature not to drive our balance into the dirt.

What should we utter over the broken glass that marks your grave?
The bird books give us mating calls but not too many death songs.
And whereas the Jews have their Kaddish and the Tibetans
have their strident prayers, all I'm impelled to do is sweet-talk
the barricades of heaven. Where you my vector
soar already, a sore thumb among the clouds.

Still I can see in the denuded maple one of last year's nests
waiting to be filled again, a ragged mass of sticks.
Soon the splintered shells will fill it
as your new geeks claim the sky — any burgling
of bloodstreams starts when something yolky breaks.
And I write this as if language could give restitution for the breakage
or make you lift your head from its quilt of wayside trash.
Or retract the mosquito's proboscis, but that's language again,
whose five-dollar words not even can unmake you.

BOB HICOK

Under construction

I meant to be taller,
I tell my tailor, who tells my teller,
who cashes my check all in ones
to suit the height of my ambition.
And kinder, I tell my trainer,
who trains my tailor and my teller too
to look better wetter and drier, kinder
to people and blue skies, moles
and Republicans, even though
it takes more muscles to smile
than tell someone to fuck off.
I ask my tuner to listen to my head
and tell me whether it sounds out of sorts;
she says a man's not a piano
and cries, for wouldn't that be nice,
a man you can sit in front of
and play like Satie turning a piano
into a river speaking to its mother,
the rain, late at night. But she's sweet,
my tuner, and tightens a few strings
in my back just to get the old tinka-tinka
up to snuff before she kisses me
on the cheek. Life. I think that's
what this is, the glow
where she smacked her lips to my skin,
birds acting surprised that the sun
has sought them out once again,
and me looking in my closet
in the morning and choosing
the suit of snails
over the suit of armor.
Who remind me to slow,
to savor, as if they know.

LEILA CHATTI

Waking after the Surgery

And just like that, I was whole again,

seam like a drawing of an eyelid closed,
gauze resting atop it like a bed

of snow laid quietly in the night
while I was somewhere or something

else, not quite dead but nearly, freer,
my self unlatched for a while as if it were

a dog I had simply released from its leash
or a balloon slipped loose from my grip

in a room with a low ceiling, my life
bouncing back within reach, my life

bounding toward me when called.

mer · cy

mer · cy *n.* **1a.** An act of divine favor or compassion; **b.** as in, 'twas *mercy* brought me from my Pagan land; **c.** 'twas grace soft as death at my mother's hands; **d.** a body on its way from one house to another. **2a.** A blessing; clemency; **b.** as in, saying politely, *I believe you have something of mine;* **c.** as in, what a mother whispers to a tree branch; **d.** as in, a razor blade that yields; **e.** the moon playing chicken with the sun. **3a.** A disposition to be kind and forgiving; **b.** as in, a prayer for sinners now and at the hour of death; **c.** as in, 'twas Jill playing jacks on the Hill; **d.** as in, mind over matter. **4a.** Something for which to be thankful; **b.** as in, a passing ship; **c.** a called game; **d.** enough food and a doorknob; **e.** a few teeth left. **5a.** Charitable treatment; **b.** as in, right before the fall; **c.** as in, ain't none of us truly free; **d.** we is all at the *mercy* of time.

JIM HARRISON

Geo-Bestiary: 34

Not how many different birds I've seen
but how many have seen me,
letting the event go unremarked
except for the quietest sense of malevolence,
dead quiet, then restarting their lives
after fear, not with song, which is reserved
for lovers, but the harsh and quizzical
chatter with which we all get by:
but if she or he passes by and the need
is felt we hear the music that transcends all fear,
and sometimes the simpler songs that greet sunrise,
rain or twilight. Here I am.
They sing what and where they are.

MATTHEW ZAPRUDER

Ceasing to Be

The idea is simple. Lucretius wanted to rid
the world of death fear by writing
On the Nature of Things. He says we fear
death only believing the mind somehow
continues even after the skull that holds it
is broken and harmless vapor leaks out
into everything dissolving. It's
true I fear my death, but I fear
the death of others more, because that's
a death without death through which
I must live. Or I fear my death
for the death others will have to live through
without me. That and probably pain
are why people are afraid. Anyway a world
without death fear would be even more scary.
Not that it matters. Death and fear. One
hand of steel, one of gold. Even you
wouldn't know which to cut off or reach
out for first, Lucretius, because it is always
very dark here in the future.

Spring

Speckled egg, brown egg, or sky blue with black marks—

Having broken once, the world re-forms
in miniature.
Over and over, in the nest
between two limbs; in the hollow of grass
at a marsh edge.

It's relentless, the way it keeps trying
to return.
Joy
Joy
Joy

RICHARD JONES

Rest.

It's so late I could cut my lights
and drive the next fifty miles
of empty interstate
by starlight,
flying along in a dream,
countryside alive with shapes and shadows,
but exit ramps lined
with eighteen-wheelers
and truckers sleeping in their cabs
make me consider pulling into a rest stop
and closing my eyes. I've done it in the past,
parking next to a family sleeping in a Chevy,
mom and dad up front, three kids in the back,
the windows slightly misted by the sleepers' breath.
But instead of resting, I'd smoke a cigarette,
play the radio low, and keep watch over
the wayfarers in the car next to me,
a strange paternal concern
and compassion for their well-being
rising up inside me.
This was before
I had children of my own,
and first felt the sharp edge of love
and anxiety whenever I tiptoed
into darkened rooms of sleep
to study the peaceful faces
of my beloved darlings. Now,
on lonely nights like this,
the fatherly feelings are so strong
the snoring truckers are lucky
I'm not standing on the running board,
tapping on the window,
asking, *Is everything okay?*

But it is. Everything's fine.
The trucks are all together, sleeping
on the gravel shoulders of exit ramps,
and the crowded rest stop I'm driving by
is a perfect oasis in the moonlight.
The way I see it, I've got a second wind
and an all-night country station on the radio.
Nothing for me to do on this road
but drive and give thanks:
I'll be home by dawn.

HEATHER MCHUGH

Everybody Has a Fatal Disease

*

In the night, while it's quiet, I run
some lips across its ribs, some eyeteeth over
knucklebones, some mind downspine.

*

The saddest dog alive could still feel love. If you must
feel a feeling, that one's fine. And if you want,
there's a refinement: feeling transitive.

*

How comfort one another,
entre nous,
and never smother.

*

Animals feel love, and then
a want is born. To feel the want
can lead to wanting feels. Some kind

of blind comparative. Comparative
of kind. (Forget superlative, that
cloying fiction: it's the index

we are always
losing touches with,
and wasting touches on.)

*

For life, o life! The time-honored
condition. (Has living any

precondition?

Is it any?)
Moments aren't
repeatable. But do endure.

    *

May I take
pictures of

your poor, afflicted
pelt? I am a well-

meaning American.

    *

Life/death:
are you insured?

It's mutual.

    *

From what is hard
to parse, or to control, or be
unimplicated by,

instinctively the lookers
turn their eyes.
The blind man has more sense.

    *

The terror in the mirror tells
of being watched. The first gaze ever met was made
a double present of. A self's a sort

of obstacle to vision.

                    *

Absurd? You hear?

                    *

To feel
(for one's own
self) one feels out
others. But with
different feelers now.
We once felt smothered, so

we have become the smotherers.

It is the counterpart of
daddy's war. This time
this is THE life, we swear.
(But life's a mother.)

                    *

Of predicaments it is
the father, too. (The DNA of

the indictment: every creature
choked with feeling.)

Life the law, the Logos.
Uncommuted! Life

the sentence.

*

Come
to grips!
Look here. Look

here! or else

I cannot read your lips.

OLENA KALYTIAK DAVIS

Not This

my god all the days we have lived thru
saying

not this
one, not this,
not now,
not yet, this week
doesn't count, was lost, this month
was shit, what a year, it sucked,
it flew, that decade was for
what? i raised my kids, they
grew i lost two pasts—i am
not made of them and they
are through.

we forget what
we remember:

each of the five
the fevered few

days we used
to fall in love.

Slow Song for Mark Rothko

1

To breathe and stretch one's arms again

to breathe through the mouth to breathe to

breathe through the mouth to utter in

the most quiet way not to whisper not to whisper

to breathe through the mouth in the most quiet way to

breathe to sing to breathe to sing to breathe

to sing the most quiet way.

To sing to light the most quiet light in darkness

radiantia radiantia singing light in darkness.

To sing as the host sings in his house.

To breathe through the mouth to breathe through the

mouth to breathe to sing to

sing in the most quiet way to

sing *the seeds in the earth breathe forth*

not to whisper *the seeds* not to whisper *in the earth*

to sing *the seeds in the earth* the most quiet way to

sing *the seeds in the earth breathe forth.*

To sing to light the most quiet light in darkness

radiant light of *seeds in the earth*

singing light in the darkness.

To sing as the host sings in his house.

To breathe through the mouth to breathe to sing

in the most quiet way not to

whisper *the seeds in the earth breathe forth*

to sing totality of *the seeds* not to eat to

sing *the seeds in the earth* to

be at ease to sing totality totality

to sing to be at ease.

To sing to light the most quiet light in darkness

be at ease with radiant *seeds*

with singing light in darkness.

To sing as the host sings in his house.

2

To breathe and stretch one's arms again

to stretch to stretch to straighten to stretch to

rise to stretch to straighten to rise

to full height not to torture not to torture to

rise to full height to give to hold out to

to give the hand to hold out the hand

to give to hold out to.

To give self-lighted flowers in the darkness

fiery saxifrage

to hold out self-lighted flowers in darkness.

To give as the host gives in his house.

To stretch to stretch to straighten to stretch to

rise to full height not to torture not to

to rise to give to hold out to

give the hand to hold out the hand to give

hope hope of hope of perfect hope of perfect rest

to give hope of perfect rest

to give to hold out to.

To give self-lighted flowers in the darkness

perfect and fiery hope

to hold out lighted flowers in darkness.

To give as the host gives in his house.

To stretch to stretch to straighten to stretch to

rise to full height not to torture to

give the hand to hold out the hand to

give hope to give hope of perfect rest to

rest not to lay flat not to lay out

to rest as *seeds* as *seeds in the earth*

to give rest to hold out to.

To give self-lighted flowers in the darkness

fiery hope of perfect rest

to hold out light flowers in darkness.

To give as the host gives in his house.

3

To breathe and stretch one's arms again

to join arm in arm to join arm in arm to

join to take to take into

to join to take into a state of intimacy

not in anger not in anger

to join arm in arm to join arms

to take into intimacy.

To take into the light in the darkness

into the excited phosphor

to be in light in the darkness.

To take as the host takes into his house.

To join arm in arm to join arm in arm to

join to take to take into

to join to take into a state of intimacy

not anger not anger

to take as *the earth* takes *seeds* as

the poor the poor must be taken into

to take into intimacy.

To take into the light in the darkness

into the phosphor star-flowers

to be in the light in the darkness.

To take as the host takes into his house.

To join arm in arm to join arm in arm to

join arms to take to take into a state of intimacy

not anger

to take as *the earth* takes *seeds* as

the poor must be taken into

to end the silence and the solitude

to take into intimacy.

To take into the light in the darkness

into star-flowers before sunrise

to be in light in the darkness.

To take as the host takes into his house.

Find the Poets

I arrived in a foreign land yesterday,
a land that has seen troubles,
    (who hasn't, you might say?).
This land
with its scrubbed white houses
and blue seas, where everything was born,
and now, everything seems as if it could vanish—
I wanted to find out the truth
about how a great land like this
could allow ancient columns to crumble
and organ grinders to disappear.

Find the poets, my friend said.
If you want to know the truth, find the poets.

But friend, where do I find the poets?
In the soccer fields,
    at the sea shore,
                in the bars, drinking?

Where do the poets live these days,
    and what do they sing about?

I looked for them in the streets of Athens,
at the flea market and by the train station,
I thought one of them might have sold me a pair of sandals.

But he did not speak to me of poetry,

only of his struggles, of how his house was taken
from him, of all the dangers his children must now
be brave enough to face.

Find the poets, my friend said.

They will not speak of the things you and I speak about.
They will not speak of economic integration
or fiscal consolidation.

They could not tell you anything
about the burden of adjustment.

But they could sit you down
and tell you how poems are born in silence
and sometimes, in moments of great noise;
of how they arrive like the rain,
unexpectedly cracking open the sky.

They will talk of love, of course,
as if it were the only thing that mattered,
about chestnut trees and mountain tops,
and how much they miss their dead fathers.

They will talk as they have been talking
for centuries, about holding the throat of life,
till all the sunsets and lies are choked out,
till only the bones of truth remain.

The poets, my friend, are where they have always been—
living in paper houses along rivers
and in forests that are disappearing.

And while you and I go on with life
remembering and forgetting,
the poets remain: singing, singing.

List of Collections

Vicente Aleixandre, "Who I Write For," from *Longing for the Light*, translated by Lewis Hyde (2007)

James Arthur, "In Praise of Noise," from *Charms Against Lightning* (2012)

Ellen Bass, "The World Has Need of You," from *Like a Beggar* (2004)

Mark Bibbins, from *13th Balloon* (2020)

Marianne Boruch, "All of Us All of Us," from *The Anti-Grief* (2019)

Jericho Brown, "Duplex," from *The Tradition* (2019)

David Budbill, "What Issa Heard," from *Moment to Moment* (1999)

Hayden Carruth, "Concerning Necessity," from *Toward the Distant Islands* (2006)

Victoria Chang, from "I Am a Miner. The Light Burns Blue," from *Obit* (2020)

Leila Chatti, "Waking after the Surgery," from *Deluge* (2020)

Lucille Clifton, "won't you celebrate with me," from *The Book of Light* (1992)

Olena Kalytiak Davis, "Not This," from *The Poem She Didn't Write and Other Poems* (2014)

Tishani Doshi, "Find the Poets," from *Girls Are Coming Out of the Woods* (2018)

Jenny George, "Spring," from *The Dream of Reason* (2018)

Dan Gerber, "Often I Imagine the Earth," from *Sailing through Cassiopeia* (2012)

Jim Harrison, "Geo-Bestiary: 34," from *Shape of the Journey* (2000)

Olav Hauge, "Anxiety," from *The Dream We Carry* (2008)

Bob Hicok, "Under construction," from *Red Rover Red Rover* (forthcoming 2021)

Hồ Xuân Hương, "Country Scene," from *Spring Essence*, translated by John Balaban (2000)

Richard Jones, "Rest.," from *The Correct Spelling & Exact Meaning* (2010)

June Jordan, "Nobody Riding the Roads Today," from *Directed by Desire* (2007)

Laura Kasischke, "Masks," from *The Infinitesimals* (2014)

Ted Kooser, "Right Hand," from *Splitting an Order* (2016)

Deborah Landau, from *Soft Targets* (2019)

Lao-tzu, from *Lao-tzu's Taoteching*, translated by Red Pine (2009)

Dana Levin, "Urgent Care," from *Banana Palace* (2016)

Heather McHugh, "Everybody Has a Fatal Disease," from *Muddy Matterhorn* (2020)

Rachel McKibbens, "letter from my heart to my brain," from *blud* (2017)

W.S. Merwin, "Rain Light," from *The Shadow of Sirius* (2009)

Pablo Neruda, "Poema 18," from *Then Come Back*, translated by Forrest Gander (2018)

Aimee Nezhukumatathil, "Love in the Time of Swine Flu," from *Oceanic* (2018)

Lisa Olstein, "A Poetics of Space," from *Late Empires* (2017)

Gregory Orr, "Not many of them, it's true," from *How Beautiful the Beloved* (2009)

Lucia Perillo, "For the First Crow with West Nile Virus to Arrive in Our State," from *Inseminating the Elephant* (2011)

Dean Rader, "Meditation on Transmission," published in the *San Francisco Chronicle* (2020)

Camille Rankine, "The Current Isolationism," from *Incorrect Merciful Impulses* (2015)

Roger Reeves, "On Visiting the Site of a Slave Massacre in Opelousas," from *King Me* (2013)

James Richardson, "Vectors 3.0: Even More Aphorisms and Ten-Second Essays," from *By the Numbers* (2010); "Vectors 4.2—Otherwise: Aphorisms and Ten-Second Essays," from *During* (2016); "Vectors 5.1—Otherwise: Aphorisms and Ten-Second Essays," from *For Now* (2020)

Alberto Ríos, "A Physics of Sudden Light," from *The Smallest Muscle in the Human Body* (2002)

Alison Rollins, "mer · cy," from *Library of Small Catastrophes* (2019)

Sarah Ruhl, "Prayer," from *44 Poems for You* (2020)

Brenda Shaughnessy, "Visitor," from *Our Andromeda* (2012)

Ruth Stone, "Goshen," from *What Love Comes To* (2010)

Anna Swir, "There Is a Light in Me," from *Talking to My Body* (1996)

Arthur Sze, "Unpacking a Globe," from *Sight Lines* (2019)

John Taggart, "Slow Song for Mark Rothko," from *Is Music* (2010)

Chase Twichell, "You, Reader, as I Imagine You," from *Things as It Is* (2018)

Jean Valentine, "Even all night long," from *Breaking the Glass* (2012)

Ocean Vuong, "Someday I'll Love Ocean Vuong," from *Night Sky with Exit Wounds* (2016)

C.D. Wright, "Obscurity and Lockdown," from *ShallCross* (2018)

Matthew Zapruder, "Ceasing to Be," from *Come On All You Ghosts* (2010)

Ghassan Zaqtan, "Fingers," *The Silence That Remains*, translated by Fady Joudah (2017)

The book you are holding is a testament to the resilience and passion of poets and poetry readers. The following individuals around the world make our work possible through their philanthropic vision and love of poetry. We are deeply grateful for your support of Copper Canyon Press. Thank you!

In memory of Brian Agler
Anonymous (6)
Scott and Sarah Armstrong
Robert Bach
Ellen Bass
Sarah Bird
Stephen Brittain
Patricia Brooke
Laurie and Bart Brown
Vincent and Jane Buck
Cindy Buhl
MaryBeth Jarvis Clark
Kim Clements/JAS Design Build
Elizabeth Coleman and
    Robert Stroup
Peter and Betsy Currie
Thomas Enochs
Lisa Every
Jenny Factor
Beroz Ferrell and Siegi Ranacher
Nancy Gifford
Kip and Stanley Greenthal
Rob Greenwood and
    Elizabeth Fetherston
Steven Holl
Lynn Hubbard
In memory of Chyrel Ann Kelsey
Sungyul Lee
Dana Levin
Mariana Lin/Jacob Lin-Sosa

Jane Ellis and Jack Litewka
Carol Lycette
Michael Joseph Mariani
Pamela Maffei and Joseph M.
    McCarthy
Dawn McGuire MD
Jana Mohr Lone and Ron Lone
Elizabeth Douglas Mornin
Jerrold Narland
Kathy O'Driscoll
Sharon L. Oriel
Stewart Parker
Linda Gerrard and
    Walter Parsons
Ella Raymond
Joseph C. Roberts
Harriett Cody and Harvey Sadis
Lucinda Santiago
In honor of Kim Seely
Dory Sheldon
Leslie Shipman
Stephen Spencer
Delphine and Charles Stevens
Bob and Katie Strong
Arthur Sze
Chase Twichell
Margaret H. Wagner
Rachel White
Sara and Ted Woolsey
Greta Zorn

Poetry is vital to language and living. Since 1972, Copper Canyon Press has published extraordinary poetry from around the world to engage the imaginations and intellects of readers, writers, booksellers, librarians, teachers, students, and donors.

WE ARE GRATEFUL FOR THE MAJOR SUPPORT PROVIDED BY:

academy of
american poets

THE PAUL G. ALLEN
FAMILY FOUNDATION

amazon literary
partnership

4
CULTURE

the point
envision·enact·evolve

Lannan

ART WORKS.

National
Endowment
for the Arts
arts.gov

WASHINGTON STATE
ARTS COMMISSION

A&
OFFICE OF ARTS & CULTURE
—— SEATTLE ——

The Witter Bynner Foundation
for Poetry